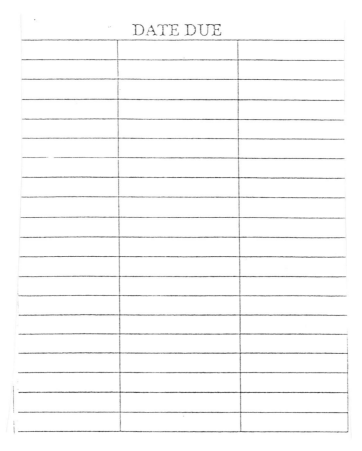

DATE DUE

SIMON COWELL:

FROM THE MAILROOM TO IDOL FAME

EXTRAORDINARY SUCCESS WITH A HIGH SCHOOL DIPLOMA OR LESS

JENNIFER ANISTON: FROM FRIENDS TO FILMS

TYRA BANKS: FROM THE RUNWAY TO THE TELEVISION SCREEN

HALLE BERRY: FROM BEAUTY QUEEN TO OSCAR WINNER

JAMES CAMERON: FROM TRUCK DRIVER TO DIRECTOR

SIMON COWELL: FROM THE MAILROOM TO IDOL FAME

ELLEN DEGENERES: FROM COMEDY CLUB TO TALK SHOW

MICHAEL DELL: FROM CHILD ENTREPRENEUR TO COMPUTER MAGNATE

STEVE JOBS: FROM APPLES TO APPS

RACHAEL RAY: FROM CANDY COUNTER TO COOKING SHOW

RUSSELL SIMMONS: FROM THE STREETS TO THE MUSIC BUSINESS

JIM SKINNER: FROM BURGERS TO THE BOARDROOM

HARRY TRUMAN: FROM FARMER TO PRESIDENT

MARK ZUCKERBERG: FROM FACEBOOK TO FAMOUS

SIMON COWELL:

FROM THE MAILROOM TO IDOL FAME

by Shaina C. Indovino

Mason Crest

SIMON COWELL: *FROM THE MAILROOM TO IDOL FAME*

Mason Crest
370 Reed Road
Broomall, Pennsylvania 19008
www.masoncrest.com

Printed and bound in the United States of America.

First printing
9 8 7 6 5 4 3 2 1

Library of Congress Cataloging-in-Publication Data

Indovino, Shaina Carmel.
  Simon Cowell : from the mailroom to Idol fame / Shaina C. Indovino.
    p. cm. — (Extraordinary success with a high school diploma or les)
  Includes index.
   ISBN 978-1-4222-2296-6 (hard cover) — ISBN 978-1-4222-2293-5 (series hardcover) — ISBN 978-1-4222-9357-7 (ebook)
  1. Cowell, Simon, 1959—-Juvenile literature. 2. Sound recording executives and producers—England—Biography—Juvenile literature. 3. American idol (Television program)—Juvenile literature. I. Title.
  ML3930.C68I53 2012
  781.64092—dc23
  [B]
                                    2011024225

Produced by Harding House Publishing Services, Inc.
www.hardinghousepages.com
Interior design by Camden Flath
Cover design by Torque + Design.

CONTENTS

INTRODUCTION

Finding a great job without a college degree is hard to do—but it's possible. In fact, more and more, going to college doesn't necessarily guarantee you a job. In the past few years, only one in four college graduates find jobs in their field. And, according to the U.S. Bureau of Labor Statistics, eight out of the ten fastest-growing jobs don't require college degrees.

But that doesn't mean these jobs are easy to get. You'll need to be willing to work hard. And you'll also need something else. The people who build a successful career without college are all passionate about their work. They're excited about it. They're committed to getting better and better at what they do. They don't just want to make money. They want to make money doing something they truly love.

So a good place for you to start is to make a list of the things you find really interesting. What excites you? What do you love doing? Is there any way you could turn that into a job?

Now talk to people who already have jobs in that field. How did they get where they are today? Did they go to college—or did they find success through some other route? Do they know anyone else you can talk to? Talk to as many people as you can to get as many perspectives as possible.

According to the U.S. Department of Labor, two out of every three jobs require on-the-job training rather than a college degree. So your next step might be to find an entry-level position in the field that interests you. Don't expect to start at the top. Be willing to learn while you work your way up from the bottom.

That's what almost all the individuals in this series of books did: they started out somewhere that probably seemed pretty distant from their end goal—but it was actually the first step in their journey. Celebrity Simon Cowell began his career working in a mailroom. Jim Skinner, who ended up running McDonald's Corporation, started out flipping burgers. World-famous cook Rachael Ray worked at a candy counter. All these people found incredible success without a college degree—but they all had a dream of where they wanted to go in life . . . and they were willing to work hard to make their dream real.

Ask yourself: Do I have a dream? Am I willing to work hard to make it come true? The answers to those questions are important!

CHAPTER 1
EARLY LIFE

Words to Know

reality television: Reality television is programming based on real people's lives or competitions that involve real people, rather than actors. Reality television shows don't use scripts.

record label: A record label is a company that finds new artists, signs a contract with them to sell their music, and then gets the word out about the artist.

borough: A borough is a smaller part of a big city. Often, large cities will be made up of several boroughs. New York City, for instance, has five boroughs.

song charts: Song charts record which songs are selling the best, ranking them by their sales.

On Monday, January 11, 2010, Simon Cowell shocked TV audiences by announcing that he would leave his job as judge on *American Idol*. The *reality television* show had been a gigantic success in the United States since it first aired in 2002, when it introduced American viewers to the sharp-tongued Simon. Based on the British show *Pop Idol*, on which Simon was also a judge, *American Idol* had made Simon Cowell an international star, mainly for his harsh criticism of the singing competition's contestants.

Simon had helped make the show a massive hit, but it was time for the television talent judge and music executive to move on. "I want to leave Idol this year bigger and better than it was in the past," he told the Television Critics Association. Simon added that he was "very proud of what the show has achieved." And he had right to be proud; *American Idol* had become one of the most popular shows on television in the time Simon was a judge on the show.

Simon wasn't leaving *American Idol* for nothing, however. He planned to start an American version of *The X-Factor*, another British reality television competition on which he was a judge. "[I] didn't think it was right to do two shows in America at the same time, so [I] decided to leave one and start another," he said. Simon was ready to get to work on something new after being on *American Idol* for almost ten years. "I'm thrilled that we have put a date on the launch of the U.S. version of *The X Factor*, and delighted to be continuing to work with Fox," Simon said. "We have a fantastic relationship, a great team and are all very excited about this."

Replacing Simon would be a major challenge for *American Idol* and for Fox, the company that aired the show. When Simon announced he would be leaving the hugely successful show, the chairman of entertainment at Fox, Peter Rice, didn't want to tell reporters who would take Simon's place on *American Idol*. Talking about finding a new judge for the show, Rice said, "We have to take our time on that. . . . We have to make sure the chemistry of the judges is as good as it could be." Simon was a unique voice

Simon's worked hard to succeed in music and television, and all without a college degree!

on *American Idol*, often the most negative judge on the show, telling contestants things they didn't want to hear, and finding someone to fill his shoes would be difficult for Fox.

Though *American Idol* was one of Simon's biggest successes, the show was just one of many amazing things he'd done in his life. Simon started his career in the mailroom of the **record label** where his father worked, and then he quickly becoming an executive there. From that point, he'd worked to create hit songs with artists in England, before joining the cast of the British show *Pop Idol*. Simon's role as judge on *American Idol* made him even more famous, allowing him to work on more projects in England and America. He'd help start shows like *X-Factor* and *America's*

On shows like American Idol *and* X-Factor, *Simon has become famous for his sometimes harsh words for contestants.*

Got Talent. With help from Simon, many of music's biggest stars got their start, including Kelly Clarkson, Carrie Underwood, and Chris Daughtry. Simon Cowell has had success in music and television, helping others become stars and making himself a star, working in front of the camera and behind the scenes.

The College Choice

What may be most surprising about Simon's rise to success in Britain and the United States is the fact that he did it all without graduating from college. Over the last few decades, the number of high school students who go on to college to continue their education has been on the rise. In 2009, for instance, 70 percent of all high school graduates went on to college the following year. That's a lot of people going to college! For many high school students, going to college after graduating is the next step on their path to a career. To become a scientist, lawyer, doctor, or teacher you'll need to have a college degree, and probably a higher degree as well (a master's or doctor's degree, as well as a bachelor's degree).

Going to college is a choice, however, and it's not for everyone. Achieving success doesn't always require a college degree, since many high school students are able to enter the workforce right after graduating. Some people know exactly what they want to do after high school, and they are ready to work hard to reach their goals. Finding work instead of going to college can be very rewarding, and it can allow you to learn many important skills while on the job.

Simon Cowell didn't go to college; in fact, he didn't even finish high school. He took a while to find what he wanted to do in life, but once Simon had set his mind to a career in the music business, he was ready to do what he needed to do in order to achieve his goals. Whether you go to college or not, there are seldom any shortcuts to achieving your career goals—it always requires hard work!

Simon's Early Life

Simon Phillip Cowell was born on October 7, 1959, to Eric Cowell and Julie Brett in the London, England, **borough** of Lambeth. Simon's father Eric worked in real estate and the music business. His mother Julie had once been a ballet dancer. When Simon was young, his father's work involved looking at places where buildings were going to be constructed and then figuring out the amount of materials needed to build them. Simon has three brothers, older brothers Michael and Tony, and younger brother Nicholas, as well as two sisters, June and Lindsay Elizabeth.

Simon grew up in the small town of Elstree, about twenty miles outside of London. He and his family lived in a house called Abbots Mead, a large home where monks once lived. Simon loved growing up at Abbots Mead. The house had four floors, eight bedrooms, and four bathrooms, plenty of space for a young Simon to play with his brothers. "For a naughty four-year-old boy," Simon wrote in his book *I Don't Mean to Be Rude, But. . .* , "Abbots Mead was the perfect place in which to grow up." Simon was often raised by nannies because his parents were always busy.

Simon grew up at a time when music was changing quickly, with new bands becoming popular in Britain and around the

The Beatles inspired Simon's start in the music business. The famous band had a massive influence on music in England and the United States during Simon's childhood.

world. In 1963, the Beatles put out their first hit, "She Loves You," to wild success. The song became number one on the pop **song charts** in England. Simon and his brothers, like so many young people, were drawn to the Beatles' rock-and-roll sound. Simon's older brother Tony bought the song, and, soon, Simon asked his mother to buy it for him as well. "It was the first time in my life that I had been interested in music; and I was desperate to own a copy," Simon wrote in his autobiography. "There was something about that music that made me sit up and listen." As someone who would go on to have great success in the music business, this was an important moment for Simon.

Simon went to boarding school for high school and got into trouble often as a teenager. In his biography, Simon wrote, "The two things I hated about school were the discipline and boredom. . . . I just had this sneaking suspicion that learning about Newton's theory wasn't actually going to play a huge part in *my* future. . . . I think it's fair to say that I was the world's worst teenager." Due to his bad behavior, Simon was kicked out of several schools. He made the decision to drop out without graduating when he was sixteen years old.

For most people, finishing high school is very important to helping them find work and start a career. Most people who drop out will have a hard time finding a job that doesn't require them

One of Simon's first jobs was working at Elstree Studios, a film studio (pictured here). Simon helped to work on The Shining.

to have graduated from high school. Luckily for Simon, his father Eric was wealthy and had many connections that would help him land on his feet after leaving school.

Early Career

After leaving high school, Simon started looking for work. His father helped him get some interviews in a variety of fields, including work at a supermarket, in a law office, and in construction, but Simon wasn't interested in any of those jobs. Often, he'd do poorly in the interviews on purpose, in order to make sure he didn't get jobs that he didn't want. Simon wasn't totally sure what it was that he did want to do, but his interest in music and entertainment continued after he dropped out.

Simon eventually got himself a job working at a movie production company near his Elstree home, Elstree Studios. Simon worked as a runner at the studio. A runner is the lowest position on a movie set; it's the person who carries props and equipment, mostly doing work that is too small and unimportant for other people on the set to do.

While Simon worked at Elstree Studios, he worked on *The Shining*, a movie based on a novel by Stephen King, starring Jack Nicholson. Simon helped clean the props during the filming of the movie. "I well remember him saying he used to clean Jack Nicholson's axe in between takes for the most famous scenes," Simon's brother Tony told BBC radio years later.

After several different jobs that didn't last long, Simon's father was able to get him a job at EMI Music Publishing, the company

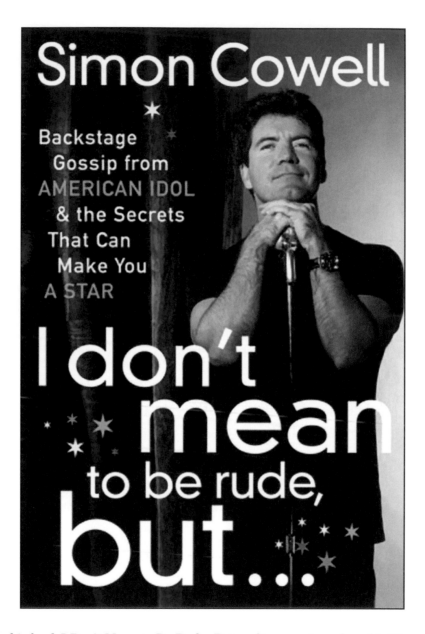

In his book I Don't Mean to Be Rude, But..., *Simon writes about his life growing up and moving into the music business.*

where Mr. Cowell worked. Simon worked in the mailroom at EMI; his job was to make sure the mail that came into the company went to the right people.

Working at EMI was Simon's first experience in the music industry, although he was far from recording songs or finding new artists, far from anything that really looked like the business of selling music. Soon, though, Simon would be working his way up from the bottom, and it wouldn't be long before he'd reach the top of the music business.

CHAPTER 2
RISE TO SUCCESS

Words to Know

repertoire: An artist's repertoire is the set of songs he has recorded and performed.

producer: A producer works with an artist to record songs.

signing: When a record label signs an artist, the company agrees to sell the artist's music and the artist agrees to only make music with that company.

single: A single is a song put out by an artist that is often the first song from an album. The single is made to help promote the artist and her album.

For many high school dropouts, finding work can be very tough, if not impossible. Simon was lucky enough to have his father get him a job at EMI Records, one of the biggest record labels in the world. He started with a very small job for sure, but it was just the chance Simon needed to break into the music business.

Life in the Music Business

Working in the mailroom was a good job for Simon—particularly because he had no real work experience, no high school diploma, and had never been to college—but it wasn't where he wanted to stay. "From my first day on the job I began planning and scheming my way to the top of the business," he writes in his biography.

The job didn't last long for Simon, and he ended up leaving the mailroom. One year later, though, he returned to EMI Music Publishing, thanks again to help from his father. Simon became an assistant to an A&R (artists and ***repertoire***) executive at the company. A&R involves finding new artists for a record company. Simon spent some time as an assistant and worked on finding new talent for EMI as well, before starting work as a ***producer***.

As a producer, Simon met Pete Waterman, who was part of famed British production team, Stock Aitken Waterman. Simon learned how to record music with Pete, as well as what makes a great song and great artist.

By 1985, Simon was ready to strike out on his own. He left EMI to start his own music publishing company with his boss from EMI, Ellis Rich. They called the company E&S Music. The company had little success, and Simon wrote in his autobiography that it was a mistake to start the company. Simon left the new company soon after it had started, but he wasn't finished.

Soon after leaving E&S, Simon met Iain Burton, and the two started a record label called Fanfare Records. Simon came to Fanfare to do A&R, just as he had for a little while at EMI. He

sought out new artists for the company and ended up **signing** Sinitta, a female singer who had worked with a dance group called
Hot Gossip. The group had worked with Burton and Arlene Phillips, a dancer whose career Burton managed, before working
with Fanfare to put out the company's first song. Sinitta was just
the artist that Fanfare needed in its early days, and just the kind
of artist who would help Simon's career as an A&R executive.

Simon knew he could make the artist a star and help her record
hit songs, but Burton was nervous about the new company. Soon,
he told Simon that he was going to back out of Fanfare. Simon
convinced Burton to give him a few thousand dollars to put out

Choreographer Arlene Phillips helped to form Hot Gossip and worked with
the group and Burton for years.

Simon found success with British pop singer Sinitta. The two also dated.

Sinitta's first *single*, "So Macho." When the song was released, it was a hit, reaching number two on the song charts in Britain. "So Macho" helped keep Fanfare in business, and Sinitta went on to have a couple more hits on the label.

Despite his early successes at Fanfare Records, Simon left the company in 1989. Without a job, he had to move back in with his parents. Simon wouldn't let his career in music end, though, and he found work with record label BMG, one of the largest in the world. Simon began putting together a label that would work with BMG to put out music from new artists. Once again, Simon was on the hunt for new talent, playing the role of A&R executive that he had at EMI and Fanfare. He called his new label S Records.

Simon began signing new artists and groups to his label, including singing groups 5ive and Westlife. Simon also made the smart decision to put out songs based on already-popular television shows, and entertainment brands. S Records released songs based on the Mighty Morphin' Power Rangers, Teletubbies, and the World Wrestling Entertainment (WWE). The songs sold very well and helped S Records become a success early on. One group on S Records, the boy band Westlife, was set for major success in Britain.

Success and Tragedy

In 1999, Simon experienced both one of the greatest achievements of his career in the music business to date and the loss of the man who'd helped him start that career, his father Eric.

Simon had been working to make his newly signed group Westlife a success in England, and by early 1999, his work was finally paying off. The group's first single "Swear It Again" had been released in March and quickly reached number one on the British song charts. Simon couldn't have been more excited about his new group's success. "Swear It Again" wasn't just Westlife's first number-one song, it was also Simon's first as a record company executive. He'd believed in the group's potential from the time he signed them to his S Records, knowing that they could be big. Simon's father felt the same way about Westlife's chance to succeed in music, so Simon wanted to make sure he let his parents know about his first number-one song.

On the day that "Swear It Again" reached number one, Simon called home to share the news. When Simon reached his mother in England, he knew something wasn't right, but he was so happy to tell her about his latest success that he kept on talking. Simon's mother called him back shortly after they got off the phone and told Simon that his father Eric had died of a heart attack. Simon was devastated by the terrible news.

Years later, Simon spoke with talk show host Piers Morgan about hearing the news of his father's death. Choking back tears Simons said,

> It wasn't, wasn't good. But you've just got to deal with it, you know, and I went back and realized that your first responsibility is that you've got to look after your mum. It was a

Westlife became a major pop act in Britain right around the time that Simon's father passed away.

horrible, horrible, horrible time, like I said. You believe everyone is going to live for ever and they don't. And all the stuff you think you care about, the hit records and stuff like that, it's just meaningless.'

Simon had lost one of the most important people in his life. His father had always been there for him, helping him to get a job when he couldn't find another, helping him move on after losing his job at Fanfare, and believing in everything he did. Simon had reached a peak in his career and a low point in his personal life on the same day. Over the next few years, Simon would continue to have success in the music business, particularly with Westlife, but learning to cope with the death of his father would take years.

Starting on *Idol*

In 2001, Simon began working on a new television show called *Pop Idol*. Created by a man named Simon Fuller, the show was going to be a singing competition where the winner was picked by the show's viewers sending in their vote by text message, phone, or the show's website. The winner of each season of the show would get a record deal, hopefully allowing them to start a successful career in music. Simon would serve as one of three judges on the show who would comment on singers' performances and help them to become better and better each week the show was on the air. The first episode of *Pop Idol* debuted on October 5, 2001, in Britain. The show was a hit, becoming hugely popular among British television viewers.

When the first season was over, the top two contestants (Will Young and Gareth Gates) won contracts with Simon's S Records. Both men went on to have success in England, scoring number-one songs. Will Young's first song on S Records sold more than 400,000 copies on its first day out, and more than one million in its first week.

After the success of *Pop Idol* in Britain, the show moved to countries around the world, with a version of the show created specifically for each country. The shows kept the same format, with three judges, viewers voting, and the same style of competition. Local versions of *Idol* became popular in Australia, Greece, Malaysia, Canada, India, New Zealand, Norway, Armenia, Vietnam, France, Iceland, and many, many other countries around the globe.

In 2002, the American version of *Idol* was shown for the first time. Called, simply, *American Idol*, the show aired on the Fox channel. Simon was hired as a judge for the new American show based on his popularity on the British version. He was known for his sharp, tough comments; he had already become a celebrity in Britain after being on the show. The American show would also have record producer and executive Randy Jackson and singer Paula Abdul filling the two other judge positions. With all the pieces in place, *American Idol* was set to become a huge success in its new home.

CHAPTER 3
IDOL BECOMES A SUCCESS

Words to Know

album: An album is a collection of an artist's songs packaged together.

timeslot: On television, a show's timeslot is the time that the show comes on. Shows in the same timeslot compete to win viewers.

American Idol came to the United States already a success in Britain. *Pop Idol* had become a phenomenon in the UK and had launched the singing careers of two of its final contestants. By mid-2002, the show was already beginning to move around the world, and America was just one of many versions of the show being produced. With Simon coming on to be a judge in the U.S. version, the show had many of the things that made the British version so popular, but it wasn't a guaranteed hit. There had been few shows like it, televised talent competitions where viewers voted on the winners. But any doubts about whether *Idol* would be a success were quickly put to the side shortly after the show debuted in the United States in the summer of 2002.

A Major Hit

When *American Idol* was first aired on June 11, 2002, just fewer than 10 million people tuned in to watch the singing competition. For the final episode of the first season, 23 million people watched the show. After singer Kelly Clarkson won the first season, the show was even more popular in its second season, during which Kelly scored a number-one debut on the **album** charts for *Thankful*, her first album. By having a winner go on to sell albums and have a successful start to her singing career, the show was proven to work, making stars out of its contestants. The second season premiere had 26 million people watching. Thirty-eight million people watched the season's final episode, in which Ruben Studdard was named the winner. The show had gone from ranked between twenty-fifth and thirtieth for its **timeslot**, to number three. Over the next few years, the show would be number one or two consistently, keeping the number of people watching around 30 million or more. From season three on, American Idol would be the number-one show for people between the ages of eighteen and forty-nine.

During this time, Simon became famous for his tough criticism of contestants. Though some thought he was rude to the singers on the show, many people liked that he wasn't telling them what they wanted to hear. Simon became the judge that many *American Idol* fans tuned in to watch, waiting to hear what would come out of his mouth next. He'd tell singers he didn't think were going to make it in the music business to stop singing and find something

American Idol host Ryan Seacrest, judge Randy Jackson, and Simon don't always see eye-to-eye on everything, but they've shared a lot of success thanks to the show.

else they did well. He'd tell people their voices were terrible, and that no amount of time could make them singing stars. When one contestant said she'd quit her job to audition for *American Idol*, he called her boss to get the woman her job back after saying she'd never make it on to the show. Simon would even jokingly say mean things about the show's host, Ryan Seacrest, and fellow judge Paula Abdul. Simon was blunt, saying exactly what he was thinking without caring what anyone thought, and his bluntness made him a star on both *Pop Idol* and *American Idol*.

Simon often began his comments on both shows by saying, "I don't mean to be rude, but. . . ," and then launching into a harsh criticism of the singing, appearance, or performance of the shows' contestants. The phrase became so associated with Simon that he used it as the title of his 2003 autobiography, *I Don't Mean to Be Rude, But. . . : Backstage Gossip from American Idol & the Secrets That Can Make You a Star.*

Creating Stars

American Idol was hugely successful, making Simon a star in the United States, but it also created stars out of the show's contestants. Many of the winners of *American Idol* have gone on to successful careers in music, some of them selling millions of albums and becoming celebrities after their appearance on the

Country megastar Carrie Underwood is just one of the many singers to come from American Idol.

show. While some have become more successful than others after *Idol*, many of the contestants on *American Idol* have made the most of the chance that the show gave them.

The winner of *Idol*'s first season, Kelly Clarkson, has gone on to be one of the most successful contestants from the show. Kelly's first album, *Thankful*, came out in 2002 to massive success. To date, the album has sold more than two million copies. *Breakaway*, her second album, cemented Kelly as a new star in music. The album sold more than six million copies in the United States and helped Kelly win two Grammys. Her huge hit "Since U Been Gone" reached number two on the *Billboard* song charts in the United States. In its first week out, Kelly's third album, *My December*, sold just fewer than 300,000 copies.

Carrie Underwood won the fourth season of *American Idol*, and she has since become one of country music's biggest stars. Her first album, *Some Hearts*, debuted at number one on the country album charts, selling more than 300,000 copies in just one week. She even returned to *American Idol* the season after she won to sing her hit song "Jesus Take the Wheel." *Some Hearts* has sold more than a million copies, earning Carrie several hit singles and many awards, including Album of the Year at the *Billboard* Music Awards. Carrie's next album, 2007's *Carnival Ride*, continued her success, giving the singer her first number-one album with sales of more than half a million copies in one week. So far, *Carnival Ride* has sold more than three million copies in the United States. *Play On*, Carrie's third album, was a massive hit too, debuting at number one on the album charts just as *Carnival Ride* had. In less than two years, the album sold just fewer than two million copies.

Chris Daughtry didn't win *American Idol*, but after leaving the show, he still became one of rock music's most successful singers. With his band Daughtry, Chris has sold millions of albums and had many hit songs. The band's first album, *Daughtry*, sold 300,000 copies in its first week. The album also gave rise to hit singles like "It's Not Over," "Home," "Over You," and "What About Now." *Daughtry* has sold over four million copies in the United States. The group's second album, called *Leave This Town*, was released in 2009 and has sold more than a million copies.

Though Kelly, Carrie, and Chris have been the most successful *American Idol* contestants, Rubben Studdard, Clay Aiken, Fantasia Barrino, Jordin Sparks, David Cook, David Archuleta, Kris Allen, and Adam Lambert have all had amazing careers in music as well. *American Idol* made them stars, but they've each made their own way after the show, working hard to make proud the people who voted for them on the show.

Syco Music and Television

In 2002, Simon started a new company that would be able to work on both music and television. He called the new company Syco. Syco Music, the record label part of Simon's new company would work under BMG, with which Simon had worked on S Records. One of the first big successes Simon had with his new label came in 2004 with the singing group Il Divo.

Il Divo has toured the world and sold millions of records with Simon's help.

In 2001, Simon had the idea to put together an international group of classical singers, because he sensed that people were becoming more and more interested in classical music and singing. He began to look around the world for singers to become part of the group, thinking that having singers from different countries around the world would give the group the widest possible appeal. Simon's search for singers ended in 2004 when he found the fourth and final member of the group. Il Divo was Spanish Carlos Marín, American David Miller, and Swiss Urs Bühler, as well as French pop music singer Sébastien Izambard. The group recorded their first album in 2004 and began to promote the

Simon has many critics, but he can take tough words as well as he can dish them out!

album around the world. The album, called *Il Divo*, was a massive hit, reaching number one on the album charts in Britain. Il Divo performed their song "Regresa a Mi" on *The Oprah Winfrey Show*, helping them to become even more popular in the United States. Around the world, Il Divo sold millions of copies of their first album and became one of the earliest successes on Simon's Syco Music.

CHAPTER 4
BRANCHING OUT

Words to Know
mentor: A mentor is someone who gives advice and helps guide another person, often someone younger or less experienced in a particular field.

With *American Idol* reaching heights that few other shows could ever hope to, Simon was ready to begin work on other projects. He realized that mixing music and television was a winning strategy, so he set to work to create other television shows that worked like *Idol*. The competition element of *Idol* had made the show a must-watch event, with viewers tuning in to see their favorites compete for the top spot. In addition, *Idol* allowed viewers to see everyday people show their talent and tell their stories. Fans loved being able to relate to a particular contestant and learn more about his or her life. Simon understood that this was a key part of why *Idol* was successful around the world, and he readied television shows under his Syco Television company that would continue to show the talents of regular people.

The X-Factor

In 2004, the television channel that aired *Pop Idol* in Britain asked Simon's company Syco Television to create a new singing competition show. Simon created a show called *The X-Factor*. The show's format is very similar to the Idol series, in that there are three judges who watch singers chosen from public auditions compete against each other for the top spot. Unlike *Idol*, each singer who makes it to the finals is assigned one of the judges to be his or her **mentor**; the judge then helps to choose songs and improve the singer's performance. The winner of each season is given a record deal, often with Simon's company Syco Music. Simon was a judge on the British version of the show, just as he had been on *Pop* and *American Idol*.

Like the *Idol* series, countries around the world have adopted *The X-Factor*, each creating their own version of the show. There have been *X-Factor* shows in Australia, the Czech Republic, Chile, Iceland, Italy, Spain, Poland, Nigeria, Kazakhstan, the United States and many other countries around the globe.

Got Talent

In 2005, Simon created another talent competition show called *Got Talent*. The show would be similar to *The X-Factor*, Simon's previous show, but would branch out from a singing competition to allow any and all talents. Whatever the contestants were good at doing, they could bring to *Got Talent*, be it singing, juggling, dancing, telling jokes, or anything else. At first, the British comedian and talk show host Paul O'Grady was getting ready to star in the British version of the show, which would be called *Paul O'Grady's*

With X-Factor, *Simon continued his streak of creating successful television shows packed with celebrities and popular music.*

Got Talent. Due to Paul's leaving the show's network that year, however, the British version of *Got Talent* was postponed. Instead, Simon worked on starting the show in the United States under the name *America's Got Talent.*

America's Got Talent was first aired in June of 2006. The show had three judges, just like *American Idol.* As performers displayed their talents, each judge had the power to either allow them to finish their act or give them an "X," voting to stop the act before its end. If all three judges voted to stop the performance, the contestant had to stop her act. At the end of each performance, the judges gave comments, saying what they did or didn't like about the act. *America's Got Talent*'s judges included

British talk show host Piers Morgan, actor David Hasselhoff, wife of Ozzy Osbourne and record executive Sharon Osbourne, and, most recently, comedian and game show host Howie Mandell. The show has been a success in the United States, and it has been on the air for six seasons. After the American version of *Got Talent* became a hit, Simon was able to take the show back to England, starting *Britain's Got Talent* in 2007.

Like *The X-Factor* and *American Idol*, the *Got Talent* series has been moved to countries around the world, with each country having its own version of the show. *Got Talent* has become popular in Albania, Australia, China, Brazil, Germany, France, Poland, Thailand, Turkey, and many other countries.

Singer Leona Lewis was the first winner of the British version of the X-Factor. *Today, she's a star around the world.*

New Stars Are Born Thanks to Simon

Just as American Idol created celebrities out of its contestants, Simon's other shows allowed regular people who just needed a chance to become stars.

In 2006, singer Leona Lewis tried out for the third season of the British version of *The X-Factor*. Simon mentored Leona during her time on the show and she ended up winning the competition that year. Simon signed her to his record label, Syco Music, and she began to work on her first recordings. Her first single sold more than half a million copies and stayed at number one on the British song charts for a month.

In 2008, the world was taken by storm by a Scottish singer in her late forties appearing on *Britain's Got Talent*. Susan Boyle sang "I Dreamed a Dream" for the judges on the show and blew them away. The YouTube video of her performance was seen by tens of millions of people around the world, and she became an instant singing star. Simon gave her a contract with Syco Music and her first album, *The Gift*, went on to sell more than 300,000 copies in a single week.

Other New Shows

The *Got Talent* and *X-Factor* series aren't the only shows Simon was working on after he'd become famous for being a judge on *Pop* and *American Idol*. He also worked to create and produce several others, continuing to mix music and television, as well as bringing regular people in front of a panel of judges for a chance to impress the world with their talent.

X-Factor *became a success in the United States in the same way* Pop Idol *succeeded as* American Idol.

In 2006, Simon produced a show called *American Inventor*, which allowed inventors from across the country to show their creation to a panel of judges who would decide on the best, most useful inventions. The judges were business people and inventors, hoping to find the next big thing among the inventions they saw on the show. Businessman Peter Jones created *American Inventor*, based on a Japanese show that allowed inventors to pitch their creations to successful business people.

Simon created a show called *Celebrity Duets* in 2006 as well. The show brought together pairs of celebrities (one singer and one non-singer) who would sing songs for a panel of judges, each week one contestant being voted off the show. Comedian Wayne Brady hosted the show, which, like *American Idol*, aired on Fox.

Simon seems to have a knack for creating shows that people want to watch and signing artists to whom people want to listen. No matter what he works on, he finds a way to make it successful. By combining television and music, Simon has found a winning formula for success and stardom. He's created new hit television shows and those shows had helped launch the careers of new music stars.

CHAPTER 5
SIMON TODAY

During his time on *American Idol,* Simon had helped make the show a success and become a star in the process. He worked to create other shows, as well, having as much success in television as he'd had in the music business, if not more. The shows he created were very popular with audiences around the world and helped to cement Simon's status as an expert in the entertainment business. But by 2010, it was time for Simon to leave the show that had made him a celebrity and brought him so much success in the United States.

Changes at *American Idol*

In January of 2010, Simon announced that the ninth season of *American Idol* would be his last on the show. He said he was ready to move on and start the American version of the show he created in Britain, *The X-Factor.* The news came as a surprise to many *Idol* fans who had watched the show for years with Simon as one of the main attractions. For some viewers, it was hard to imagine *American Idol* without Simon Cowell as one of the show's judges. A year before, singer Paula Abdul had left the show, being replaced by comedian and talk-show host Ellen Degeneres. The show had also added music executive and song-writer Kara DioGuardi, bringing the number of judges to four. But with Simon leaving the show, the show needed to make some major changes to keep fans interested. The show's first season without Simon would be its tenth and by that time, fans were looking for something new from the popular show.

In order to keep fans happy, the show brought on new judges. Randy Jackson, a favorite of *American Idol* fans, stayed on for the tenth season, but Ellen and Kara left the show. Replacing Simon, Ellen, and Kara were singers Jennifer Lopez and Steven Tyler, lead singer of the rock group Aerosmith. The show was back to having just three judges.

Despite Simon leaving the show and the many changes to the judging lineup, *American Idol* remains one of the most successful television shows of all time. The show has had more viewers than any other in American history according the **Nielsen ratings**. In addition, the show is the only one to have remained the most viewed show in its timeslot for six straight years. Comedy shows *All in the Family* and *The Cosby Show* were each in the top spot for five years straight, but *American Idol* topped them both, a feat no other show has achieved.

New Opportunities for Simon

Before he left *American Idol*, Simon worked on bringing his British show *The X-Factor* to the United States. When he announced that he was leaving *Idol*, he also announced the beginning of his new show, one that his company Syco had helped create in Britain years before. The American version of the show debuted in September of 2011 on the Fox network, the company that had brought *Idol* to American television. The American version of *X-Factor* became a huge hit, another success in a long line of them for Simon. He'd planned to be working on both the American and British versions of *X-Factor*. In early 2011, however, reporters confirmed that Simon wouldn't stay on as a weekly judge at the British version of the show, instead focusing on the American version while working on the British version mostly from behind the scenes. At the end of 2010, Simon also signed on to continue his work as a judge on *Britain's Got Talent* until around 2013.

While he worked on new projects on television, Simon was also making changes in his personal life. In February 2010, Simon asked his girlfriend Mezghan Hussainy to marry him. She said yes, and the two were engaged to be married. Mezghan was a makeup artist on the set of *American Idol* when the two met and started dating.

Giving Back

Many people may think that Simon is rude and even mean, and he'll be the first to admit that he can be—but he's also concerned with making sure that he uses his success to help other people.

Simon's been involved in a number of causes for charity. He's worked with PETA (People for the Ethical Treatment of Animals) to create advertisements warning against leaving pets in a hot car and speaking against wearing fur. One ad has a picture of Simon holding a dog saying, "If you wouldn't wear your dog, please don't wear any fur." Simon's also been involved in charities committed to children's health and making sure sick kids are cared for in the best possible way. He's known for inviting children from the Association of Children's Hospices backstage when he's working on *The X-Factor.*

In 2010, British Prime Minister Gordon Brown asked Simon to record a song with famous singers and musicians to help victims of the January 2010 earthquake in Haiti. Money made from

Simon worked hard to organize the charity single "Everybody Hurts" after the 2010 earthquakes in Haiti.

sales of the song would go to charities devoted to rebuilding Haiti and helping those who had been affected by the disaster. Simon was only too happy to help the people of Haiti with the single. He chose the R.E.M. song "Everybody Hurts," and asked celebrity singers to sing on the song. Singers from Britain and the United States helped to record the song, including many of the stars whose careers Simon had helped start. Leona Lewis, Susan Boyle, and members of the pop group Westlife all lent their voices to the "Helping Haiti" single. Miley Cyrus, James Blunt, Michael Buble, Jon Bon Jovi, Mariah Carey, Robbie Williams, and Kylie Minogue also sang on the song. The song was a huge hit, selling almost half a million copies in one week and reaching the top of the pop song charts in Britain. The charity version of "Everybody Hurts" was also a hit in countries around the world, including Ireland, Australia, Germany, New Zealand, Switzerland, Spain, and Canada, among others. Most important of all, the money the song made went straight to help the people of Haiti.

Still Successful

Today, Simon Cowell is more successful than ever. After working on *American Idol*, one of the most successful television shows of all time, Simon is branching out to work on other projects in both television and music. He's had a hand in creating some of the music world's biggest stars, and making some of the most popular television shows of the last decade.

Simon's success comes from his drive to work hard and from his no-nonsense attitude. Though his critical comments may make him seem prickly or even unlikeable, Simon understands that the music business can be just as harsh as the things he says to talent competition contestants. His sharp tongue has helped him become popular on television as someone people love to hate, though Simon's fans respect his judgments as advice from someone who knows the entertainment business well.

Simon told *Business Week* that in order to become a success in business it's important to "work hard, be patient, and be a sponge while learning your business." He continued, "Learn how to take criticism. Follow your gut instincts and don't compromise." Simon has certainly shown himself to have the drive needed to reach his goals, particularly when he started his career without graduating high school. Simon's smart decisions come out of years of experience in the music industry and an understanding that entertainment is a business. "I've always treated the music business as a business," he told *Business Week*. "Whether I'm making TV shows or signing artists, you have to do it by the head and not the heart—and I run my businesses that way."

Few people can say they've done as much, or achieved the same level of success as Simon. On the *Daily Telegraph*'s 2008 list of the 100 most powerful people in British culture, Simon's was ranked as number six. In 2010, *Time* magazine named Simon one of their 100 most influential people in the world. Nick Cannon, host of *America's Got Talent*, wrote a **tribute** to Simon in the magazine. Simon may not always be the warmest person on television, but there's no doubting that he's reached heights that many others strive to reach.

And he did it all without having gone to college!

Melanie Amaro won the first season of the American version of X-Factor in 2011.

WHAT CAN YOU EXPECT?

Of course not everyone who skips college is going to be a celebrity or a millionaire. But there are other more ordinary jobs out there for people who choose to go a different route from college. Here's what you can expect to make in 100 of the top-paying jobs available to someone who has only a high school diploma. (If you're not sure what any of the jobs are, look them up on the Internet to find out more about them.) Keep in mind that these are average salaries; a beginning worker will likely make much less, while someone with many more years of experience could make much more. Also, remember that wages for the same jobs vary somewhat in different parts of the country.

Position	Average Annual Salary
rotary drill operators (oil & gas)	$59,560
commercial divers	$58,060
railroad conductors & yardmasters	$54,900
chemical plant & system operators	$54,010
real estate sales agents	$53,100
subway & streetcar operators	$52,800
postal service clerks	$51,670
pile-driver operators	$51,410
railroad brake, signal & switch operators	$49,600

brickmasons & blockmasons	$49,250
postal service mail carriers	$48,940
gaming supervisors	$48,920
postal service mail sorters & processors	$48,260
gas compressor & gas pumping station operators	$47,860
roof bolters (mining)	$47,750
forest fire fighters	$47,270
private detectives & investigators	$47,130
tapers	$46,880
continuous mining machine operators	$46,680
rail car repairers	$46,430
shuttle car operators	$46,400
rail-track laying & maintenance equipment operators	$46,000
chemical equipment operators & tenders	$45,100
explosives workers (ordnance handling experts & blasters)	$45,030
makeup artists (theatrical & performance)	$45,010
sheet metal workers	$44,890
managers/supervisors of landscaping & groundskeeping workers	$44,080
loading machine operators (underground mining)	$43,970
rough carpenters	$43,640

derrick operators (oil & gas)	$43,590
flight attendants	$43,350
refractory materials repairers (except brickmasons)	$43,310
production, planning & expediting clerks	$43,260
mine cutting & channeling machine operators	$43,120
fabric & apparel patternmakers	$42,940
service unit operators (oil, gas, & mining)	$42,690
tile & marble setters	$42,450
paperhangers	$42,310
bridge & lock tenders	$41,630
hoist & winch operators	$41,620
carpet installers	$41,560
pump operators (except wellhead pumpers)	$41,490
terrazzo workers & finishers	$41,360
plasterers & stucco masons	$41,260
painters (transportation equipment)	$41,220
automotive body & related repairers	$41,020
hazardous materials removal workers	$40,270
bailiffs	$40,240
wellhead pumpers	$40,210
maintenance workers (machinery)	$39,570
truck drivers (heavy & tractor-trailer)	$39,260

floor layers (except carpet, wood & hard tiles)	$39,190
managers of retail sales workers	$39,130
cargo & freight agents	$38,940
metal-refining furnace operators & tenders	$38,830
excavating & loading machine and dragline operators	$38,540
separating, filtering, clarifying & still machine operators	$38,450
motorboat operators	$38,390
dredge operators	$38,330
lay-out workers (metal & plastic)	$38,240
forest fire inspectors & prevention specialists	$38,180
medical & clinical laboratory technicians	$37,860
tire builders	$37,830
dental laboratory technicians	$37,690
paving, surfacing & tamping equipment operators	$37,660
locksmiths & safe repairers	$37,550
sailors & marine oilers	$37,310
dispatchers (except police, fire & ambulance)	$37,310
pipelayers	$37,040
helpers (extraction workers)	$36,870

rolling machine setters, operators & tenders	$36,670
welders, cutters & welder fitters	$36,630
solderers & brazers	$36,630
gem & diamond workers	$36,620
police, fire & ambulance dispatchers	$36,470
models	$36,420
meter readers (utilities)	$36,400
mechanical door repairers	$36,270
public address system & other announcers	$36,130
rail yard engineers, dinkey operators & hostlers	$36,090
bus drivers (transit & intercity)	$35,990
insurance policy processing clerks	$35,740
insurance claims clerks	$35,740
computer-controlled machine tool operators (metal and plastic)	$35,570
license clerks	$35,570
court clerks	$35,570
fallers	$35,570
septic tank servicers & sewer pipe cleaners	$35,470
parking enforcement workers	$35,360
highway maintenance workers	$35,310
floor sanders & finishers	$35,140

tool grinders, filers, & sharpeners	$35,110
paper goods machine setters, operators & tenders	$35,040
printing machine operators	$35,030
inspectors, testers, sorters, samplers & weighers	$34,840
pourers & casters (metal)	$34,760
loan interviewers & clerks	$34,670
furnace, kiln, oven, drier & kettle operators & tenders	$34,410
recreational vehicle service technicians	$34,320
roustabouts (oil & gas)	$34,190

Source: Bureau of Labor Statistics, U.S. Department of Labor, 2008.

Find Out More

In Books

Cowell, Simon. *I Don't Mean to Be Rude, But. . . : Backstage Gossip from American Idol & the Secrets That Can Make You a Star.* New York: Broadway Books, 2003.

Cowell, Tony. *The Secret Diary of Simon Cowell.* London: JR Books, 2009.

Newky-Burden, Chas. *Simon Cowell: The Unauthorized Biography.* London: Michael O' Mara Books, 2009.

On the Internet

International Movie Database Page for Simon Cowell
www.imdb.com/name/nm1101562/bio

People.com's Biography of Simon Cowell
www.people.com/people/simon_cowell/biography

Simon Cowell Biography
www.biography.com/articles/Simon-Cowell-10073482

Simon Cowell—Music Mogul Millionaire
entrepreneurs.about.com/od/famousentrepreneurs/p/simoncowell.htm

Index

Picture Credits

Aaron Settipane / Dreamstime.com: p. 33
Broadway Books: p. 18
Carrienelson1 / Dreamstime.com: p. 8, 30, 40, 43
Damslattery: p. 16
David Fowler / Dreamstime.com: p. 24
Imagecollect / Dreamstime.com: p. 27
Luckydoor | Dreamstime.com: p. 15
Mira Argon: p. 46
Sbukley / Dreamstime.com: p. 11, 12, 20, 38, 44, 48, 54
Sry85: p. 37
Syco Music: p. 52
the_diet_starts_monday: p. 34
Wolfgang Webster: p 23

To the best knowledge of the publisher, all images not specifically credited are in the public domain. If any image has been inadvertently uncredited, please notify Harding House Publishing Services, 220 Front Street, Vestal, New York 13850, so that credit can be given in future printings.

About the Author

Shaina Carmel Indovino is a writer and illustrator living in Nesconset, New York. She graduated from Binghamton University, where she received degrees in sociology and English.